The Fantastic Life of Elvis Presley

CONTENTS

1	The Fantastic Life of Elvis Presley	3
2	The Woman Behind Elvis	15
3	The Man Behind Elvis	27
4	"Everything Sure Is C-r-a-z-y!"	35
5	The Story Elvis Doesn't Want Told	47
6	Why Elvis Is Often Lonely	55
7	Elvis Personally Answers His Critics	62
8	Things You Never Knew About Elvis	70

Original publication dates:

The Fantastic Life of Elvis Presley
The Elvis Presley Story, 1960

The Woman Behind Elvis
The Elvis Presley Story, 1960

The Man Behind Elvis
Movieland magazine, April 1957

"Everything Sure Is C-r-a-z-y!"
Movieland magazine, June 1957

The Story Elvis Doesn't Want Told
Movieland and TV Time magazine, May 1959

Why Elvis Is Often Lonely
Movieland magazine, March 1958

Elvis Personally Answers His Critics
Movieland magazine, May 1957

Things You Never Knew About Elvis
Movieland and TV Time magazine, February 1959

Copyright © 1957, 1958, 1959, 1960 by Hillman Periodicals
ISBN: 978-1535123952

A. J. Cornell Publications

1 THE FANTASTIC LIFE OF ELVIS PRESLEY
by James Gregory

It's a strange feeling to hear yourself on a record with Elvis Presley. Strange, but thrilling.

I know, because I had the privilege of "cutting a record" with Elvis. Not a musical record, not one of the fabulous Gold Records with which he cut a bright swath across the entertainment world. But this particular record means a great deal to me—and, I suspect, to Elvis.

The record is called "Elvis Sails." One side is a recording of Elvis's final press conference before leaving for Germany on September 22, 1958, and the other includes his farewell to his U.S. fans. I am one of the writers and editors whose voices are heard asking Elvis questions on his final day in the United States, at the Brooklyn Army Terminal, where the

Navy transport U.S.S. *Randall* was waiting to carry him to Germany.

Why do I feel that record is an important one in the fantastic life of Elvis Presley? Not only because it was made on a memorable day in his life, but primarily because—in his answer to one of my questions—Elvis revealed what seems to me to be most important in his life: his devotion to his late mother, and his dedication to the high ideals she instilled in him as a child. His mother lives on in Elvis through those ideals.

You can hear our words on the record....

"Elvis," I told him, "the readers of our magazine asked me to pass along their sympathy to you in the recent death of your mother. And I wonder if you'd like to say a few words of tribute to the way she's helped you in your life."

"Yes, Sir," Elvis replied, "I certainly would....

"Everyone loves their mother. But I was the only child, and Mother was always right with me all my life. And it wasn't only like losing a mother. It was like losing a friend, a companion, someone to talk to. I could wake her up any hour of the night, and if I was worried or troubled about something—well, she'd get up and try to help me.

"I used to get very angry at her when I was growing up. It's a natural thing. When a young person wants to go somewhere or do something and your mother won't let you, you think, 'Why, what's wrong with *you?*' But then, later on in the years, you find out and you know that she was right—that she was only doing it to protect you, and keep you from getting in any trouble or getting hurt.

"And I'm very happy that she was kind of strict on me—very happy that it worked out the way it did," Elvis concluded.

Yes, Elvis is glad things worked out the way they did—that he had the stern but loving upbringing that his mother gave him.

Sternness was an easy thing to come by in the Depression years into which Elvis Presley was born. But love—then as always—was rare and to be cherished. All his life Elvis was to cherish the love his mother and father lavished on him, a love that made him feel wanted and secure despite the poverty that threatened his family throughout his early years.

Elvis Aron Presley was born January 8, 1935, in Tupelo, Mississippi, the son of Gladys and Vernon Presley. As his mother put it, "We had twins, and we matched their names—Jesse Garon and Elvis Aron. Jesse died when he was born. Maybe that is why Elvis is so dear to us." But it wasn't the only reason. From earliest childhood, Elvis was the kind of boy any parent could be proud of—quiet, well-behaved, and yet all boy.

The Presleys had little money. Vernon worked as a sharecropper, and Gladys took a factory job to help out.

Elvis's family was always deeply religious. And one of his earliest memories is of singing with his father and mother in the First Assembly Church of God in Tupelo. "When Elvis was just a little fellow, not more than two years old," Gladys Presley recalled later, "he would slide off my lap, run down the aisle, and scramble up to the platform. He would stand looking up at the choir and try to sing with them. He was too little to know the words, of course, but he could carry the tune." And so Elvis's first public "performances" were in church, singing the Gospel songs his friends and family loved.

Before long, the three Presleys—little Elvis flanked by his proud parents—were a popular vocal trio at all kinds of church affairs, ranging from camp meetings to conventions. They were much in demand at revival meetings, where Elvis's piping voice could be heard raised in song, high and clear and unafraid, above his parents' deeper tones.

In the schools of Tupelo—even the public schools—it was customary to begin the day with a brief devotion. On two mornings, Elvis's fifth-grade teacher, Mrs. J. C. Grimes, asked if any of the children in her class could say a prayer. There was no answer until the third day. On that day Elvis raised his hand. Not only did he say a prayer, but he also sang several of the songs he had learned from his parents. Mrs. Grimes was so thrilled by Elvis's beautiful voice that she told his mother about the incident, and she also told the principal, Mr. Cole, about it.

Before long, Gladys Presley received a note from Mr. Cole inviting Elvis to enter a music contest at the coming Alabama-Mississippi fair. Elvis decided to go.

As his mother recalled later, "Elvis sang 'Old Shep.' Well, he was last on the program, and the time ran out, but he was the one the crowd wanted, so they gave him the prize. We were all happy about Elvis being able to sing that way in front of 5,000 people."

Elvis's father was so delighted with his son's voice that he bought him a guitar.

"He always liked the guitar best of all his things," his mother recalled later. "That pleased me, because he'd be content to sit in front of the radio picking out melodies, or play the phonograph, trying to learn the songs he heard. The house was always full of kids, but I didn't care how many, or how much noise they made, as long as I knew they were all right and happy—that they weren't getting hurt or into mischief."

The Presleys moved to Memphis, Tennessee, when Elvis was 13, and there he attended L. C. Humes High School. One of his classmates, George Klein, an announcer at radio station WKEM, Memphis, who had been editor of the school paper and president of the senior class, says: "I remember exactly when Elvis first drew my attention. We were singing Christmas carols. And you know, it's funny— I can't tell you who else was appearing on that particular program, but I do know what Elvis did. He sang 'Cold, Cold, Icy Fingers.' That was a popular tune in the country-western field. I never forgot it. There was just something about the way he sang that always stayed with me."

A teacher recalls that Elvis was "a gentle, obedient boy and he always went out of his way to do what you asked him to do. He was a boy who needed friends, and he made them. He had a warm, sunny quality about him that always made people respond."

After a difficult period of searching, Elvis's father had found a fairly good job in Memphis, and his mother held a variety of jobs to add to the family finances. Elvis himself began to help the family, starting with a $14-a-week job as an usher at Loew's State theatre. In 1953 he graduated from high school and took a job driving a truck for the Crown Electric Company, bringing home about $35 a week. It seemed like big money then.

At about that time, Elvis decided to give his mother something special for her birthday—a record of his voice. So he went to the Sun Record Company in Memphis, paid $4.00 and cut his record.

Sam Phillips, the president of Sun Records, heard Elvis singing and recognized that the boy had possibilities. He took Elvis's name and told him he might call him back later for an audition. Elvis then put the record under his arm and carried it home to his mother, who was delighted with it. The record was called "That's All Right, Mama," and Elvis still has it, though it's pretty well worn out by now.

Elvis heard no more from Sam Phillips for a year. Then, one day, Phillips called, hurried him into a recording session, and had him cut "That's All Right,

Mama" backed by "Blue Moon of Kentucky" for his company. Elvis left with a contract.

The record was released in the summer of 1954. The night it was to be played over Memphis station WHBQ, Elvis slipped out to a movie and hid, afraid his friends would laugh at him. But while Elvis was at the movies, fame came knocking. The station received 14 telegrams and 47 phone calls during the three-hour broadcast, and disc jockey Dewey Phillips had to play Elvis's record seven times. In the week that followed, 7,000 copies of the record were sold in Memphis.

After the initial excitement had died down, this first record failed to become a big seller at the time. But it did draw enough attention to persuade Colonel Tom Parker to sign on as Elvis's business manager. Colonel Parker also signed guitarist Scotty Moore and bass player Bill Black.

In the fall of 1954, Elvis was touring the country areas as "The Hillbilly Cat" when he was booked to appear at the annual convention of the Country and Western Disc Jockeys Association in Nashville, Tennessee. There Steve Sholes, chief of RCA Victor's specialties division, heard Elvis sing. Sholes had kept track of Elvis since hearing his first record, "That's All Right, Mama," and now he saw that Elvis had developed his own style.

Sholes went to Sam Phillips, who still had Elvis under contract, and found that Phillips had several unreleased recordings that Elvis had made. For $35,000—a record-breaking sum for a new, untried artist—RCA Victor obtained all five masters of Elvis's records from Phillips. And as a bonus for signing with Victor, Elvis received $5,000, with which he promptly bought his first Cadillac.

Ever since the day he heard Elvis's very first record, Steve Sholes has been one of his biggest boosters. He recently pointed out to *Movieland and TV Time* that Elvis is "a natural talent. He's never studied singing or music. Just picked them up. He's got a greater variety of style than most people give him credit for. He can sound great on a hymn as well as on rock 'n' roll or a ballad."

Now that it had Elvis under contract, RCA Victor pressed all five of his records under its own label and released them all at once—again, something unheard of in the record industry.

Elvis's first national TV appearance soon followed. He was seen on Jackie Gleason's *Stage Show* with Tommy and Jimmy Dorsey, and sang "Heartbreak Hotel." By the time Elvis had finished making six weekly appearances on *Stage Show,* his recording of "Heartbreak Hotel" had become the number one record all over the country, his other records had become hits, and Elvis himself was the talk of show business. Wherever he went for his terrifically successful personal appearances, he was greeted by crowds of fans.

Elvis then flew to Hollywood for a screen test and appeared on the Milton Berle show. Some of the critics didn't like the unique style of his performance, especially the free-swinging movement that is so natural and exciting a part of his style, and from then on he was often the subject of critical barbs. But the people, millions of them, loved his performances and made him a new national idol. They realized that his singing and his movements were simply the clean and natural expression of a young man's exuberance—a young man so full of the joy of youth that he couldn't help expressing it in his songs.

Elvis appeared on the Steve Allen show the following July, and two weeks later Ed Sullivan signed him at a total of $50,000 for three appearances. His screen test was a huge success and Hal Wallis inked him to a seven-year, one-picture-a-year, non-exclusive contract. But his first movie, *Love Me Tender,* was made for another producer, at 20th Century Fox. Its opening on November 15, 1956, at the New York Paramount was heralded by a mammoth cutout of Elvis strumming his guitar, which was unveiled with great fanfare and stood overlooking Times Square as a symbol of many film successes to come.

Loving You, Elvis's second movie, was a great success, as were all four of his pictures. It was released in June 1957 by Hal Wallis–Paramount and was followed in November 1957 by *Jailhouse Rock,* which Elvis made at MGM. His final picture before entering the Army was *King Creole,* another Hal Wallis production, released by Paramount in June 1958. In *King Creole,* most fans and critics feel, Elvis gave his finest performance.

While fame was lavishing its rewards on Elvis Presley, he never forgot the mother and father whose sacrifices had made it all possible. He bought his parents a beautiful green-and-white ranch house in the center of a large lot in Memphis, surrounded by green lawn and trees. And when his fame and wealth increased, he moved them into an elegant $100,000 mansion, "Graceland," where Gladys Presley was a gracious and beloved hostess to all his friends—the buddies from his early days who became his trusted companions, and the girl friends who flocked to Elvis but always failed to win his heart on any permanent basis. For his best girl, as he always said, was his mother.

Elvis's parents found themselves suddenly thrust into the limelight, with their son a national celebrity. And while they enjoyed Elvis's fame and were grateful for it, sometimes it was almost too much for them. "Mom and Dad never got over all these people," Elvis said. "Mom heard me on the radio all day around the house and I told her just not to get tired of it because that's a good sign. She and Dad used to come to all my shows within a hundred miles or so of Memphis, but I didn't want them traveling further than that. In one way, Mama couldn't take it very well.

"She was down in Florida one time when the girls started to mob me," Elvis recalled with a smile, "and they started to yank my clothes off. Mama thought they were hurting me—pulling me apart or something. Shucks, they were only tearing my clothes—I don't mind it a bit!" Elvis didn't mind, for he knew it was only a sign of his fantastic popularity.

And then, at the height of his success as an entertainer, with a yearly income in the millions, Elvis was drafted into the Army. And just as be had been a great entertainer, he determined to be an equally good soldier, doing his duty and asking no special favors. In this he has succeeded remarkably.

Elvis was inducted into the United States Army at Memphis, Tennessee, on March 24, 1958, and arrived at Fort Chaffee, Arkansas, to begin his reception processing that night. He then went to Fort Hood, Texas, for training.

While Elvis was at Fort Hood, the greatest tragedy of his life occurred. His beloved mother took sick and, after Elvis had made a flying trip home to visit her bedside, she died on August 14, 1958, at the age of 42, the victim of a heart attack brought on by hepatitis.

Elvis and his father were both heartbroken. But, ever the good soldier, after the funeral Elvis returned to Fort Hood and took up his duties again. And barely a month later, on September 22, 1958, he was shipped to Germany to serve as a jeep driver. He brought his father to Germany to live with him in a rented house near his base.

When I saw Elvis at the dock the day he sailed for Germany, he had been on a crowded troop train for three days and two nights, and his heart was still heavy with the ache of his mother's death. But his greeting to me, to the many reporters who flocked to his press conference, and to the fans who leaned over fences straining for a glimpse of him, was as warm and friendly as it could be. Nobody who meets Elvis Presley can help liking and admiring him, for the secret of his greatness as an entertainer is simply his great humanity—the warmth and understanding that flow from him in a great wave to the far shores of the world, bringing music and laughter and love for all who have ears to hear.

And now, as he completes his two years of service in the Army, Elvis must know that his fans still remember, with gratitude, all the pleasure he has brought into our lives. And he must know, too, that there will be a warm place of welcome for him when he comes to gladden our hearts once again with his songs.

2 THE WOMAN BEHIND ELVIS

When Elvis Presley said goodbye to his beloved mother early in 1958 and went off to serve in the Army, his thoughts already leapt ahead to his happy homecoming in the spring of 1960. But that homecoming is marred by a shadow—the shadow of Gladys Presley's death in the summer of 1958, a few weeks before Elvis sailed for Germany.

Now, returning from Germany to his beloved native land, Elvis can't help thinking of his mother—mourning her unforgotten death, but thinking too of the timeless gift she gave him—the gift of her love, a gift he'll never forget. At this time of homecoming, this time of return to the scenes of his past, here is the story of the one girl Elvis will really remember more than any other as he comes back to America. . . .

Poverty was Elvis Presley's birthright.

But the fact of being poor, desperately "sharecropper poor" in the red clay hills of Tupelo, Mississippi, during the stark days of the Depression, never ripped his family apart as it did so many others.

Instead, their lack of material goods nurtured a feeling of love between Elvis and his father and mother that grew stronger when better, happier days came to pass. The love came simply, stemming from the realization that they had no one but each other.

Times were bitterly hard when Vernon Presley and Gladys Smith were married in 1933. Vernon was 18, a handsome young farmer. His new bride was 17, lighthearted and gay.

Their thoughts were of each other, not of the black Depression that held the country in a stranglehold. And when it was learned that Mrs. Presley was expecting twins, their joy overcame the fact that getting enough to eat was much more difficult than it is now.

The new father-to-be "farmed on shares"; that is, he tilled land owned by someone else for a share of the profits. Those profits were extremely small, and the work was long and hard, but Mr. Presley drove himself, knowing that soon he would be working for four—not two.

Then tragedy joined hands with poverty in the Presley household. One of their twin sons was born dead. The heartbroken parents named the surviving baby Elvis Aron, and lavished the love reserved for two on the tiny infant.

As Elvis grew to toddler size in Tupelo, his parents sought to provide for themselves and their son. Mr. Presley continued to farm, while Mrs. Presley worked in the small Tupelo clothing factories. Despite their labors and the constant, all-enclosing poverty, the Presleys became a sharing, loving family group.

In later years, Elvis spoke of it this way: "I like to do what I can for my folks. We didn't have nothin' before—nothin' but a hard way to go."

The Presleys moved to Memphis before Elvis started to school, in hopes of finding a better life. But times in the big city were as hard as in the country, and Mr. Presley had trouble finding a job.

"There were a lot of days when I would go out looking for jobs and get discouraged," Mr. Presley says. "I always knew if I could get back home to Gladys, everything would be all right. She would always say, 'Things will get better.' "

The family lived in a public housing project where rent was low and everybody in the building was in the same financial situation. Mrs. Presley worked as a waitress, a hospital nurse's aide, and at various other positions. Still, she managed to keep a good home for her husband and her boy. City records show she was labeled a "neat" housekeeper.

Elvis realized he was not as fortunate as other children. Instead of brooding, he tried to help. While still very young, he would tell his mother: "Mama, someday I'm going to buy you all the things you want, and we'll never be poor again."

And Mrs. Presley, smiling with tears in her eyes, would hug her son close to her and say, "I know you will, Darling. Now go on outside and play."

With the lifting of the Depression, life became a little better in the Presley household. Elvis was in school, Mr. Presley had obtained a steady job, and Mrs. Presley continued to be the devoted wife and loving mother. Elvis was quiet to strangers and classmates—not shy, but there was little time for friends.

Music had always been a part of Elvis's life. It started in church, where the little boy was an enthusiastic singer of the old hymns. His dad bought him a guitar with the few dollars of his savings, and Elvis began to strum the hymns and folk songs heard in church and at home.

Elvis had a constant companion in his guitar. He even took it to school, and spent many a lunch hour and recess learning new chords and trying them out in new tunes he had picked up. Throughout it all, there was that rhythm—an inborn, God-given rhythm yet unrecognized, nevertheless still there, dominating his playing and singing.

Mr. and Mrs. Presley listened to the youngster, encouraged him, and secretly were proud of their son's talent, like all parents whose children love and work at a thing that is close to their hearts.

When Elvis was old enough to obtain a job, he quickly began to contribute to the family income. Though he had a strong love for athletics, and football stood at the top of the list, he had to pass it up to attend to the more important task of making a living.

After high school, Elvis found full-time employment as a truck driver with an electrical appliance company. His father worked in a paint factory. The Presleys had moved out of the housing project, but expenses were higher and income still low. Elvis's salary was only around $35 a week.

He wanted to give his mother something extra-special for her birthday after he got his new job, but the decision was hard for the teenager to make. Finally he hit on a surprise—"Why not make a record of my voice?"

So when Elvis came into Sam Phillips' small recording studio to make a birthday record for his mother, he had his entire week's salary in his hand. He was nervous, but didn't let his nervousness stop him from squaring off in front of the microphone, raising his guitar, and doing the song that caused Phillips to note down his name and put it on file.

Mrs. Presley was pleasantly surprised at her son's birthday gift. But she was even more surprised at the chain of events that followed.

Phillips called Elvis back to do a commercial record, and this time Elvis got paid for it instead of having to pay for it out of his own pocket. Its title was "That's All Right, Mama."

What happened next has been told hundreds of times in newspapers and magazines throughout the world. There were many more record dates, personal appearances, television shows, movies—and within three years Elvis Presley was the idol of millions and an immensely wealthy young man.

In the space of those three years, Elvis had come from a poor truck driver to the nation's best-known entertainer. Money, once so scarce, had now become so plentiful that it was possible to buy everything he ever dreamed of—and much, much more.

The first thing he did was to move his parents into a comfortable $40,000 home in one of the city's better residential districts. His mother would never again have to keep house in a public housing project. He built a swimming pool, loaded the garage with expensive cars, and filled the home with laborsaving appliances and luxuries.

His parents were happy and thrilled over their son's rise to fame and fortune. They were content to live in their new home, visit with their friends, and stay in the background of his success.

But some of Elvis's fans would not let the Presleys live as ordinary, well-to-do people. They rang the doorbell at all hours of the day and night, blocked his driveway so that nobody could drive in or out, pulled up grass from his lawn to keep as souvenirs, and even clustered around his bedroom window and disturbed his sleep.

Mr. and Mrs. Presley made the best of this, but it was obvious that things could not go on this way. Mrs. Presley, once genial and pleasant to everyone, now became shy and kept inside the house.

Elvis realized that his success had hurt his parents' privacy, and this worried him. So he bought a big $100,000 white-pillared mansion in a suburb south of the city, put up a high stone wall, and after spending several thousand dollars on redecoration, moved his mother and father into their new home.

The big home was often vacant. Elvis, eager to have his parents near him, arranged for them to accompany him on his trips whenever circumstances would permit.

Once, while making a movie in Hollywood, he rented a home and after a day in front of the cameras would return to his parents each night.

"I just enjoy having my family around," Elvis once said. "I don't look at it as just a duty—something I ought to do. I love them and like them and I like to have them around. They can't be replaced. They're all I've got in the world.

"Doesn't everybody feel the same way?"

When Elvis was drafted, he made only one statement showing hesitancy about going into the Army. It wasn't that he minded giving up a multi-million-dollar career for two years, or being without the worship of his fans. He didn't want to leave his mother.

"I guess the only thing I hate about going into the Army is leaving Mama," he said. "She's always been my best girl."

And she really was Elvis's "best girl." Mrs. Presley personally met many of the girls he dated, and Elvis made it a point to ask each current "flame" to visit at his home in Memphis. Mrs. Presley had long talks with the girls, telling them of her son's early, less fortunate life, and of his devotion to home and family.

After Elvis went into the Army and finished basic training, the Presleys joined him several times at his camp at Fort Hood, Texas. It was known that Elvis would be sent to Germany after finishing advanced training, and several times he spoke of asking his family to accompany him overseas.

But this was not to be.

While on a visit to see her son, Mrs. Presley became ill. She returned to Memphis, and the family doctor immediately had her hospitalized. Her malady was diagnosed as hepatitis, or "yellow jaundice," a disease that attacks the liver. Four specialists were called in, and after three days, the family physician called Elvis's commanding officer, requesting that he be granted emergency leave.

Elvis, terribly worried, disobeyed his mother's wish that he not travel by airplane and rushed to her bedside. When he arrived he was pale and haggard, and brushed past fans at the hospital entrance to enter his mother's room.

"Oh, my son, my son," Mrs. Presley said as Elvis entered her room. They embraced, and when Elvis came out into the corridor, he had tears in his eyes.

"Mama's not doing very well right now, not well at all," he said.

He spent the next day—all of it—in his mother's room. Her spirits were raised by his presence, and when he left for home that night he promised he would take home some of the flowers she had received from many of his fans. Mr. Presley was spending the night at the hospital.

The telephone's ring woke Elvis from his sleep at 3:15 the next morning. The voice at the other end of the line gave the news that plunged the nation's most popular entertainer into helpless, heart-rending grief.

His mother, who had led Elvis along his path to success with wise counsel and deep love, had passed away of a heart attack brought on by her sickness. She was 42 years old.

Elvis, numbed by shock, raced to the hospital. He met his father, who by his tears confirmed the news of his mother's death. Then, father and son together retired in seclusion behind the iron gates of the big mansion.

Friends rallied to aid the heartbroken men. Col. Tom Parker, Elvis's manager, was quickly notified and flew to Memphis. Anita Wood, Elvis's steadiest date at the time, received the news as she prepared to make a national TV appearance. After the performance, she caught a late plane in New York for Memphis. Cliff Gleaves, Elvis's best friend, was on the Florida nightclub circuit. He arranged a leave of absence to come to his friend's side.

It was nearly noon before Elvis and his father came from their house, sobbing, to sit together on the front steps.

"She's all we lived for," Elvis said. "It just couldn't

be true. She was the most wonderful mother anyone could ever have. She was always so kind and good."

"She's gone, she's not coming back; everything is gone now," Mr. Presley murmured.

And father and son embraced each other in their grief.

Elvis looked down the mansion's circular driveway.

"I remember, when she felt bad, we'd walk with her down the driveway to help her feel better," he said.

"Now she's gone forever."

It was first decided to hold the funeral in the home, but the plans were cancelled on the advice of Col. Parker.

"Elvis said his mother loved all his fans," Parker said. "He wanted them to have a last chance to see her."

So the funeral was held in the chapel of a downtown funeral home, open to the public. Over a thousand persons passed by the bier to pay their last respects, and many more crowded outside, unable to enter.

The services were conducted by the Rev. James E. Hamill, pastor of the First Assembly of God Church where Elvis and his family had attended for so many years. When Elvis arrived at the funeral home, he had to be helped from the car by two men. He was limp with grief, as was his father. Elvis sat in a side room with about 30 other friends and relatives, shielded by a curtain from the congregation in the chapel.

Rev. Hamill pointed out that Mrs. Presley had fulfilled her duties as a wife and mother.

"Women can succeed in most any field these days, but the most important job of all is being a good wife and a good mother. Mrs. Presley was such a woman," Rev. Hamill said.

"I would be foolish to tell this father and son, 'Don't worry, don't grieve, don't be sorrowful.' Of course you will miss her. But I can say, with Paul, 'Sorrow not as those who have no hope.'

"If these people did not believe in God, my job would be much harder. But they have a firm belief in God, and know there is a life after death."

During the service, the famous Blackwood Brothers Quartet sang several hymns, including Mrs. Presley's favorite, "Take My Hand, Precious Lord."

The graveside service was short. About 50 policemen kept the estimated 700 onlookers well back from the family. Again Elvis had to be helped from the car.

After the final prayer, Elvis was assisted to his feet. Half-fainting, he leaned on the casket and moaned, "Oh, God, everything I have is gone. Goodbye, Darling, goodbye. I loved you so much."

Flowers had come from everywhere—from stage and screen personalities, friends, and from many fan clubs. There were remembrances from Marlon Brando, Sammy Davis Jr., Dean Martin, Ricky Nelson and Ernie Ford, among others.

And Elvis's Army friends had not forgotten him.

There were cards from all ranks of the Army, from private to general, expressing condolences.

Army authorities had granted Elvis an extension of his emergency leave, so he could be alone with his father. Elvis came down with a slight virus the day after the funeral, and was put to bed for a day.

The rest of his leave was spent quietly, in company with his father and close friends at home. He was not seen outside the grounds, and the lights in the big house on the hill burned very late each night.

Elvis Presley had lost the person dearest to his heart. His sorrow is still there. But time and his mother's teachings are helping to heal the ache.

It's almost certain that Elvis, even when his sorrow was greatest, could hear his mother say, as she said long ago:

"Things will get better." And if she were alive now to welcome her son home from the Army, she could say with pride and truthfulness: "Well done, Elvis."

3 THE MAN BEHIND ELVIS

When the house lights of the theatre dim or the TV master of ceremonies announces, "America's singing sensation, Elvis Presley," and the screams from the young teenage fans subside, it is doubtful that any of Elvis's millions of fans do more than settle back to savor each throbbing note of his liquid Southern voice and each beat of the pulsating rhythms of his guitar.

It is certain that few of them ponder on the remarkably parallel career of another young man, who rose from the obscurity of the waterfront of Hoboken, New Jersey, to capture the hearts and imaginations of their older sisters. The young man was Frank Sinatra. It's peculiarly fitting that "Frank Sinatra's Welcome Home Party for Elvis Presley," scheduled for 8:30-9:30 p.m. EST Sunday, May 8, 1960, over the ABC Television Network, should be the occasion for Elvis's return to TV after his Army service.

Few of their fans know or care that in addition to their undeniable talents, both Frank and Elvis share a blessing in still another way. Behind the careers of both is another man. In each instance, it was this man's shrewd judgment and Solomon-like decisions that did so much to skyrocket them to the top of the heap in show business.

Sinatra's aide was George Evans, a bespectacled man who had wandered into New York's Paramount Theatre late one afternoon in 1943 and had watched Frank perform in his first solo appearance since his departure from Tommy Dorsey's band. Although Frank wasn't setting the world on fire, Evans at once caught the magnetism that flowed across the footlights into the hearts of the audience. It was Evans who dreamed up the headline-grabbing stunts that put the name Frank Sinatra on the tongues of everyone throughout the USA. It was Evans who thrust Frank into the company of business tycoons and Presidents. It was Evans who guided Sinatra through a stormy personal life until his own untimely death in 1951.

The divine power that supplied Sinatra with his George Evans has graced Elvis Presley with the same sort of guiding genius. His name is Colonel Tom Parker.

No one will ever know the private thoughts of Colonel Tom Parker the balmy spring night he wandered into an auditorium to hear Elvis for the first time. Suffice it to say he must have had much the same feeling that George Evans had when he first heard Sinatra. The frenzied roar of hundreds of teenagers must have stirred a long dormant feeling in the Colonel's breast. It brought back the memories of his many years with carnivals and the circus. Once again he could hear the discordant music of the calliope, the smell of freshly roasted peanuts and the booming voice of the midway barker calling, "Hur-ry, Hur-ry, Hur-ry!"

The Colonel, as he is called—though the title is an honorary one—is quite a man in his own right. A heavy-set man with thinning hair, the Colonel was born in 1909. His past life is not too clearly defined, nor is it ever likely to be until and unless the Colonel gets around to it. He much prefers to talk about his favorite subject, Elvis Presley. He eats, sleeps and dreams Presley and fights tooth and nail to get the best for his boy.

Since descending on the Hollywood scene, he has established himself as a wit, a homespun sage and a man with an eagle eye for the welfare of his client. Many have likened him to the late Will Rogers because of his apt observations on the world at large. The laugh lines around the eyes in the Colonel's craggy countenance are concrete proof that this is a man who considers the world his own private domain and a man who is determined to squeeze every ounce of pleasure from it.

The saga of the Colonel in Hollywood is an amazing one. He has fenced with the shrewdest brains in the business and, in just about every instance, gotten exactly what he wanted for Elvis. Anecdotes about him began to circulate the moment he first alighted from a plane at Los Angeles International Airport and gazed at the surrounding countryside. Here was another oyster from which he intended to pluck the pearl.

During the shooting of Elvis's first film at 20th Century Fox, the Colonel was approached by a producer on the lot who suggested that since Elvis's picture was about finished, he would consider it a great favor if the Colonel allowed Elvis to sing two songs in his own picture, then in production. The Colonel said that would suit him just fine—but just how much money did the producer intend to pay Elvis? The producer replied that he would rather have the Colonel tell him how much Elvis would expect for the job, which would only take two days to complete. With a bland expression the Colonel said, "$75,000." The producer almost fainted. When he recovered his composure, he fairly screamed, "$75,000 for two days' work? You must be crazy!"

"No, Son," replied the Colonel, "that's what we want but I'll tell you what I'll do. Since $75,000 seems too much for you, I'll make it easy for you. I'll match you—double or nothing."

People may think the Colonel has an extraordinary viewpoint, but they must admire a man who has the full courage of his convictions.

All the contracts are drawn by the Colonel and are considered classics by some of the best legal brains in the industry. There is no fine print in a Presley contract. As a matter of fact, all of them are printed in block letters at least one inch tall to prevent anyone's saying at a later date that they misunderstood the fine print. As the Colonel puts it, "All anyone has to do to understand our contract is be able to read."

The Colonel interprets everything Elvis does in terms of "How much money does it pay?" Ernest Borgnine, who was making *Three Brave Men* at 20th the same time Elvis was filming *Love Me Tender*, became fast friends with both Elvis and the Colonel. Ernie, with a chuckle, tells of the morning the Colonel and he were lounging in front of Ernie's dressing room casually discussing the affairs of the day. A representative of a national publication told the Colonel, with undisguised enthusiasm, that the magazine was prepared to do a story on Elvis. The Colonel fixed him with a steady stare and said, "That's mighty nice of you, young man, but tell me one thing—do you want the abbreviated $2,500 version or the full-length $5,000 story?"

It is this unorthodox approach to life and the complexities of making a living that tend to place the Colonel in that select group which faces even the most serious problems of life with the complete disdain of those who have inner peace and the knowledge that we travel along the road of life but once, and are, therefore, determined to pause and smell the flowers as they pass.

One of the most amusing tales concerning the Colonel's complete disregard for precedent involves a top-ranking TV show (not a variety show) which visits with celebrities. The Colonel was approached by the show's co-producers with the suggestion that Elvis be a guest on the show. The Colonel was agreeable until he discovered that the appearance was to be without compensation. The Colonel was aghast—but not for long. Calmly puffing his big cigar, he said, "Gentlemen, you really mean you get all the top stars in the entertainment world to appear under such conditions?"

"Of course," they replied. "They do it for prestige."

"Well, let's examine the picture," the Colonel continued. Turning to each of the producers he asked, "Do you get paid for your work on the show?"

Each replied, "Yes."

"And the commentator," continued Colonel Parker, "he gets paid, too?"

"Yes," the co-producers replied, not without impatience.

"Tell me one more thing," Colonel Parker pursued. "You do have a sponsor who picks up the tab for the whole show, don't you?"

"Yes," they replied wearily, "but everyone appears on the show for prestige."

"You mean everyone gets paid on the show but

my poor boy, Elvis?" the Colonel said, thunderstruck.

"Well," said the co-producers somewhat defensively, "how come all the other people do this for nothing?"

"That's easy," said the Colonel with a grin. "It's like I've always said: 'What some people need is a good manager.'"

Such pixie-like, tongue-in-cheek comments have made the Colonel virtually a legendary character in the eyes of the smart money boys in Hollywood. Only one or two items puzzle some of these people. "How can Elvis afford all those cars—since he is in such a high income tax group?" they ask. If, they reason, Elvis bought all the cars and he has been known to gross more than a million a year, he could easily be in the 80 to 90 percent income tax bracket. And this would mean, automatically, that Elvis would have to earn many thousands of dollars more than the cost of the cars—to come out even! Though they don't understand such expenditures, they figure the Colonel must know whether or not Elvis can afford to and/or should have those cars. To date he hasn't made any costly or ill-advised career or financial moves on Elvis's behalf. We doubt that he will, either.

Some veterans wonder, too, why Elvis's TV appearances have specialized, it would seem, in close-up rather than full-length shots. They insist that there is nothing more suggestive about Elvis's singing style than that of any of the East Indian dances which are so popular on TV variety shows. So why should anyone keep him in close-up so much of the time?

Whether or not such a speculation is valid is a moot point. Only one thing is certain and of importance: Most smart show people bow low in the direction of Elvis and particularly of Colonel Tom Parker, a man who has swept across the Hollywood skies like a breath of fresh air. He has truly brought back to show business a large slice of that intangible called glamour. He's also made Parker advice spell millions for Elvis Presley.

4 "EVERYTHING SURE IS C-R-A-Z-Y!"

One evening in Hollywood, as Elvis Presley left the set of *Loving You,* he headed his shiny Cadillac toward a Paramount side street exit. As usual, however, since Elvis had started his picture, the street was teeming with teenagers, who appear everywhere Elvis goes.

As he stopped the car to sign autographs, Elvis kidded with the girls. "What do you do for a living?" he cajoled a seventh-grader. Then he happened to glance into his rearview mirror. What he saw there made him nudge his cousin, Gene Smith, to look, too, and give reassurance that Elvis wasn't dreaming.

Completely surrounding the back of the vehicle were several teenagers, busily gliding their hands back and forth across the body of the car, gathering particles of dust. Then they carefully transferred the powdery accumulation from their fingers into envelopes.

If Elvis and Gene were momentarily puzzled, the explanation was simple to Elvis's followers. To them, a pinch of Presley's car dust is a tangible substitute for Elvis's stardust, and collecting it had become the latest whim of some Presley fans.

"Crazy, man," Elvis smiled at his cousin. "Everything sure is c-r-a-z-y!"

He was referring, of course, to the five-ring circus his life has become. And to Gene, remembering Elvis's uncomplicated existence in Tupelo, Mississippi, and Memphis only a few years ago, and all that's happened since, this must have sounded like the understatement of the year.

Even in the service, Elvis's popularity has led to all kinds of fantastic occurrences.

Ever since he hit the Big Time, the most unexpected things have been happening to Elvis in fast succession. Frank Sinatra experienced much of the same a decade ago, with bobbysoxers swooning when he sang. Only in later years it was disclosed that in the beginning, some of the fainting Sinatra fans were part of a publicity stunt dreamed up by his press agent. With Elvis, the mass adulation is far too great, too real and too omnipresent to be engineered by anyone pulling strings behind the scenes for publicity.

It's difficult today for Elvis to remember when he first realized that he probably would never lead any semblance of a normal life again. The reasons against it mushroomed too fast, snowballed into an avalanche without warning, and the momentum shows no signs of diminishing.

Enjoying a meal in a restaurant is now almost out of the question. Some fans and the curious have been known to surround Elvis's table, pluck at the buttons on his jacket and stare at each morsel he raises to his lips. It can be just as bad when he dates a girl. There's no such thing as privacy for Elvis, even though he takes his date to a movie. Once when he took a young lady to a picture in Memphis, while Elvis was inside his feminine fans scrawled love messages in lipstick on his white Cadillac!

It's the price of fame, he's been told. Yet does anyone ever get used to holding a bear by the tail and not being able to let go?

How Elvis is keeping the delicate balance of the merry-go-round that is his life today, yet holding his own two feet planted firmly on the ground, is all the more remarkable when we look at some of the more amazing episodes in his daily life.

During the last presidential election, for instance, several write-in votes were cast for Elvis for President.

In Chicago, a 200-pound hog named Elvis was adjudged Champion Barrow in the junior feeding contest at the International Livestock Exposition.

Seldom a week passes that some mother doesn't write Elvis that she's named her newborn baby after him.

The biggest Hollywood stars find excuses to stop by his table at the studio commissary and wrangle an introduction when Elvis is making a picture. Dean Martin, for instance, brought his son Dino to Paramount especially to meet Elvis, but added as he left for a recording session, "Can I borrow hit?"

"I don't dance," Elvis once told a reporter. "I don't know how." And within 24 hours he received a gift certificate to learn at any one of a well-known chain of ballroom dance studios. (There was one amusing hitch, we're told, however: the gift lessons extended only to the waltz.)

At Paramount, he was assigned to Academy Award winner Anna Magnani's dressing room and given a bicycle with "Hound Dog" printed on it.

Regardless of where he is, his telephone calls from all over the world average one every five minutes. Elvis used to take them all until it became a physical impossibility to answer the phone and work, too.

When pretty blonde starlet Gail Land proved so anxious to work with Elvis in *Loving You* that she offered to forego her salary, she was hired. But, of course, she was paid. Her first day's salary went for a Presley portable phonograph and Elvis's albums.

Unfortunately, however, all the things that are happening to Elvis are not always light and humorous.

Because he's a topic of conversation everywhere, practically every entertainer considers his act incomplete without a takeoff on Elvis's unique style. While Elvis was in Las Vegas, he watched headliners in no less than six of the hotels spoofing him in their acts.

The satires ranged from mildly amusing to acid-sharp. If Elvis objected, however, no one learned it from him. Perhaps he was thinking that imitation is the highest form of flattery. Or, what's the use of objecting and setting off a new controversy when he finds himself unavoidably in the middle of so many without a move from him?

One of the few times he's raised his voice in protest, however, was over the label that sometimes accompanies his name. "I don't like being called "'the Pelvis,' " he said. "Would you?"

The magic name of Elvis Presley continues to make headlines, even when the subject matter is beyond his control. But on occasion, when he hasn't been there to speak for himself, happily there were others to do it for him. He found an unsuspected champion in a Culver City, California, rabbi who rose to defend him after a Los Angeles judge publicly criticized Elvis's hairstyle and the singer himself.

"Parents who rave and rant when Presley appears," said the rabbi, "are using him for a scapegoat and whipping boy for their own failures in bringing up their children. On the other hand," he went on, "Elvis symbolizes youthful success: a stable of high-powered multi-colored motor cars, the adulation of girls and an audience of millions. This is the stuff of which adolescent dreams are made," he concluded. "What's so wicked about it?"

As complicated and turbulent as Elvis's life has become, it is ironic that he had more freedom of movement in Hollywood than in his native Memphis. The answer is that in Hollywood Elvis was but one celebrity—albeit an important one—in a community of many famous people. As a result he is not so much of a novelty in Hollywood as in Memphis. His life at home, by comparison, is a roller-coaster ride that never stops, and once his rocketing fame brought an unprecedented move by his neighbors.

It had been building up since Elvis bought his parents a home on fashionable Audubon Drive, had a swimming pool installed and erected an iron fence decorated with musical notes. In short order, what used to he a quiet residential street became as busy as a Memphis thoroughfare.

Finally the neighbors, all of whom liked the Presleys but were weary of the increased traffic, crowds and general confusion that follows Elvis everywhere, even to his home, organized a committee to call at Elvis's home. Their proposition was simple and straight to the point: If the Presleys would consider selling their home, the neighbors would chip in and buy it on the spot.

Elvis was out of town at the time, but when he returned and learned of the proposal he was furious. He had nothing to do with the crowds collecting, he reasoned. They were more of an inconvenience to him and his parents than to the neighbors. But what could he do?

"Why didn't you ask them," he said to his father, "what they wanted for all their houses? Maybe I'll buy them out, instead."

When Elvis is in Hollywood, he has his fans and his public wherever he goes. But his life is on more of an even keel than when he's on the road or at home. While making *Loving You,* his headquarters were at the Knickerbocker Hotel, only a block from Hollywood and Vine. Because of the large staff Elvis has collected, the hotel had to assign nearly the entire 11th floor to his party.

Not the least important of the Presley entourage were the three young musicians who always back Elvis on records—D. J. Fontans, Bill Blake and Scotty Moore. They were in *Loving You* and between assignments Tab Hunter selected them to supply the musical background for the recordings he was making in his new singing career.

At the hotel, when in Hollywood, Elvis often uses the service elevator to avoid the crowds in the lobby. But once he reaches his suite high in the sky, there are no fans peering in the windows and his leisure moments are his to enjoy.

"It's safer," declares Elvis, explaining why he spends so much time in his rooms. "Less chance of getting into trouble. I like my success very much and am grateful, but I now appreciate what it is to walk on the street and go where you want without being stopped. Some of them tear your clothing and, of course, there's always the guy who makes insulting remarks, looking for a fight."

For all these reasons, Elvis, his cousin, his musicians and a few friends, both male and female, usually spend their evenings in Hollywood sitting around, preparing special dishes they like, watching TV or playing records. The girls often bring favorite records from their collections to entertain Elvis, and the sessions generally conclude with the playing of some of Elvis's own recordings, including those not yet released.

He calls his home in Memphis most every night when in Hollywood, and sometimes calls girls he's met while on tour in various cities and talks at great length. Unlike when he's on the road and playing shows at midnight, then stays up till sun-up, in Hollywood Elvis turns in early, because he has to be at the studio between 7 and 8 a.m.

Sometimes, when he tires of the hotel confinement, Elvis goes out, usually to a movie.

One night he attended a studio screening of *Gunfight at the O.K. Corral*, produced by his employer, Hal Wallis. He caused a few eyebrows to raise when he applauded wildly and loudly as Hal Wallis's name was flashed on the screen. But Elvis's demonstration was in no sense a means of buttering up his producer. He was honestly enthusiastic about seeing a familiar name in the list of screen credits.

He was equally as uninhibited in his enthusiasm when he met Cecil B. DeMille and the veteran producer asked Elvis if he'd seen *The Ten Commandments* and how he liked it.

"Crazy, man!" said Elvis, slapping the venerable

Mr. DeMille on the back. "Real crazy."

His earnings are fabulous, yet the truth about them and his relations with his mentor have been exaggerated and distorted.

A printed item which hinted that Elvis and his manager were at odds over certain matters, and that Elvis had suggested certain changes, brought a prompt and decisive telegraphic denial from Elvis. On the contrary, he declared, he is very happy with Colonel Tom Parker as his personal manager. And as for the rumors about their wrangling over finances, he added, the Colonel turns Elvis's earnings over to Papa Presley, who keeps the books.

In 1956, for instance, his earnings were nearer one million dollars (before taxes) instead of the three million reported. When he's appearing on the road for one-nighters it is not uncommon for Elvis to earn $50,000 a week. In addition, his take is approximately four cents on each of his recordings sold, and the 32 products marketed by his own Presley Enterprises increases his earnings even more.

It's an amusing but unconfirmed report that those "I Love Elvis" and "I Hate Elvis" buttons are made by the same company—Elvis's—and that he collects on both.

If the Colonel is Elvis Presley's best insurance against anyone taking advantage of him, he is also Elvis's most qualified booster and defender against his critics. They've been together since the start.

"Elvis," the Colonel insists, "doesn't rock 'n' roll.

When teenagers listen to him (he doesn't play for dances) they sit in their seats and soon begin to jump. And that's what his music should be called—Sit 'n' Jump.

"He doesn't bump or grind—he undulates and the undulations come naturally. The music goes 'round and 'round and Elvis goes 'round with it. However, the undulating bit is purely incidental. It doesn't sell songs but it helps.

"As for this Elvis-the-Pelvis stuff, just let me say this: Everybody has a pelvis."

It is noteworthy that those who become closely associated with Elvis—those who get to know him best—become as big Presley boosters as his colorful manager. Joe Gray, Elvis's stand-in, had never seen Elvis until they met on a sound stage. Now he's a Presley fan, too, for reasons all his own.

"That Presley name is like magic," says Gray. "I'm going great with dames. I tell one I'm Elvis Presley's stand-in and I don't have to do any more pitching. She's the one who asks me if I want to go for a cup of coffee. Now, I'm beginning to appreciate Presley's appeal ... wow! Seriously, though, he's a great guy, and I've worked with the best. I never expected him to be so regular, and I can smell a phony. Presley is nice, courteous to everyone. To me, the crew, the fellows and the girls."

Any way you look at it, the wonderful life of Elvis Presley is a turbulent one, filled with surprises, upheavals and constant change. But those who know him best say that the most amazing of all Elvis's qualities is his ability to adjust himself readily to new situations, whatever they are.

His secret is profiting by his experiences, rather than brushing them off.

There was a time, for instance, when Elvis would pose for his picture with anyone who asked him. No more. He learned the hard way that too many people were selfishly trying to exploit him.

"I sat down with one girl I'd known a long time back home in Memphis," he recounts, "and sort of rested my head on her shoulder. You know what happened? She sued me when the picture was printed. Colonel Parker settled it out of court for $5,000."

Since then, Elvis has become so leery of posing for photos with the many who ask him that once, more from habit than the situation at hand, he politely declined to be photographed with Jayne Mansfield and her muscleman, Mickey Hargitay, when a photographer approached the trio vacationing in Las Vegas.

Because he'd been criticized in some quarters for wearing clothes some think extreme, Elvis listened, thought it over, and again profited by the experience. The result is that while he hasn't discarded the attire he wears while performing, he's made some changes in his regular wardrobe. When he arrived in Hollywood for a movie, he visited a smart haberdasher and ordered dozens of plain jackets and shirts, save for one white leather shirt.

Elvis's life is full of changes, and there are many

more lying ahead. But if he sticks to his homespun philosophy, he has nothing to worry about.

"A person can do just about anything he wants to do," Elvis once said. "If you really try," he added thoughtfully, "the Good Lord won't let you down."

Even when everything goes c-r-a-z-y.

5 THE STORY ELVIS DOESN'T WANT TOLD

Many big-name stars in show business make it a point to "cash in" on the things they do to help others.

Wherever they give a benefit performance, or appear on a charity show, or take part in a national drive of some sort, they make sure that the story gets to the newspapers and magazines.

The publicity that comes from these so-called "public service" appearances is often more valuable than if they were getting paid for it.

Other stars are different. They do charitable things with no publicity, and take as their reward that wonderful feeling of being able to contribute to someone else's welfare.

That is the story Elvis Presley doesn't want told. For he is the second kind of star.

But since he is in the Army, serving his country just like any other young man with a duty to perform, the story of his unpublicized good works and generosity has to be told.

Elvis very likely wouldn't want this article to be published.

He's like that—modest, and possessed with a great inner desire to make people happy.

But the deeds must come out. Not only the big things that he has done for many, but the little, relatively unimportant episodes that have made a few persons truly know what Elvis Presley really is.

Many don't know that at the moment, a municipal park bearing Elvis's name is under construction at his birthplace, Tupelo, Mississippi. The park is being built on the site of Elvis's Tupelo home, where he lived before moving to Memphis when he was 13.

It all began in the summer of 1956, when Elvis appeared at a show in Tupelo.

While he was at the show, city officials mentioned to Elvis that the town had no facilities where children could play safely, no playground equipment for them to use.

Right then, Elvis pledged to Tupelo mayor James F. Ballard and others that he would do his part to make the "hill land" behind his birthplace into a park that would furnish recreational facilities for Tupelo youth.

The following fall, Elvis went back to Tupelo. He was between movies—he needed a rest. But because of that pledge, and the fact that people were counting on him, he made a guest appearance at the Tupelo fair.

Of course, the place was packed, but Elvis didn't get a nickel for his services. Every cent of the proceeds, more than $20,000 in all, went to the Elvis Presley Municipal Park.

Mayor Ballard, in outlining the plans of the 12-acre park, said: "It will include first-class park facilities which the city could not afford to give Elvis and his friends when they were growing up."

Other people caught the spirit of Elvis's generosity. Contributions poured in, construction firms in Mississippi and Tennessee donated equipment and labor to clear and level the park site.

In the future, the park will become a $250,000 recreation area, big enough to enable children from all over north Mississippi to benefit from it.

Mayor Ballard put it simply when he said, "This is just another example of the way Elvis has used his talents and fame in helping his fellow men."

Nobody really knows how many times Elvis has appeared onstage, often unannounced, to help out somebody or some cause. A few are remembered.

There is the time he sang for half an hour (and captivated the audience) in front of a crowd of over 14,000 in the Memphis baseball park. Two Memphis charities got over $6,000 each for that one.

Or the time he made an unscheduled appearance at a show for Danny Thomas's pet project—the St.

Jude Hospital for Children. Elvis just walked onstage, with no prior announcement, and told the audience he came "just because I thought I should."

Elvis knows that the St. Jude Hospital, to be built in Memphis, will be used for the treatment and research of rare childhood diseases, chiefly the dreaded killer, leukemia. All children of every race and creed will be treated there.

Children, especially small ones, affect Elvis tremendously. Perhaps he remembers his own childhood, when things weren't very easy. Whatever the reason, youngsters make him do more things than fame or dollars would ever do.

Scotty Moore, Elvis's guitarist, recalls an incident in Shreveport, Louisiana:

"It was the Christmas season," Scotty said, "and we were driving around town one afternoon before a performance. We weren't doing anything special, just out for air and a look at the city.

"Suddenly Elvis said, 'Wait a minute—see those little girls selling Christmas cards on the street? Turn around.'"

"So we went back. Elvis looked at a couple of boxes of the cards. Then he said, 'I'll take 'em all.' There must have been a thousand of them. They're probably still out at his house."

The story of Cheryl Hart is another episode that bears out the fact of Elvis's love for children. We wish it could have been a happy story.

Cheryl was an 11-year-old girl from Schenectady,

New York, doomed to die of aplastic anemia.

During the last few weeks of her illness, Cheryl wanted more than anything else to have an autographed personal picture of Elvis.

Elvis was home on furlough from his basic training in Texas. Word of Cheryl and her wish got to him somehow.

He immediately airmailed his picture to the little girl in the hospital at Albany, New York. Written on it was the message:

"To Cheryl, God Bless You, Elvis."

Cheryl lived two weeks after receiving the picture. Doctors said the picture, and the message, caused her to respond noticeably.

This may have been a very small thing in the life of many, but it wasn't to Elvis. He knew that his picture meant more to a dying child than all other things in the world.

The city of Memphis has perhaps benefited more by Elvis's generosity than any other place. It is not highly publicized, but since reaching the top Elvis has been making substantial contributions to city charities, especially the Christmas food funds.

Even during Christmas in 1958, Elvis didn't forget, though he was overseas and just back from two tough weeks on field maneuvers. Two $1,000 checks bearing Elvis's signature were received by each of the two funds.

The Memphis Zoo, also, has been aided. Elvis, like most all small boys, liked to go to the zoo. He probably went as often as he could, mainly because it wasn't too far from his home, and also because no admission was charged.

Friends and fans from all over the world have sent him animals since he became a famous figure. Elvis was grateful for the gifts, but he knew they would be cared for much better, and give more pleasure to more people, if they were put in the zoo where all could see them.

Monkeys, birds, and even an Australian wallaby (similar to a kangaroo) have been some of Elvis's gifts to the zoo.

Elvis combined his love of football with support for a favorite cause in the fall of 1957. Each year, a Memphis civic group sponsors a high school football game for the benefit of blind persons in the city and county. From the money, each sightless person receives a check at Christmas.

So Elvis bought tickets for the entire student body of his high school—1,400 tickets, which cost him over a thousand dollars. He bought them, even though he couldn't go to the game himself. He had tried it the year before, and his appearance had almost caused a riot among the fans. He had to leave before seeing a single play.

Elvis never got to play football in high school because he had to quit the team to go to work. "I used to lie awake nights and dream of being a football hero," he has said. "I lived football—it's still my favorite game."

Personal gifts from Elvis to friends, acquaintances, and girls he dates have been numerous, and without much publicity. Elvis just likes to do things for people.

Blonde Anita Wood, Elvis's steadiest date when he is home, is a recipient of many gifts from him. They represent Elvis's feeling of loving to give, and the close friendship the two share for each other.

One of his most lavish gifts to Anita was a ring, containing a big diamond surrounded by 18 sapphires. Anita wears it now—on the third finger of her *right* hand.

As a going-away present when he went into the Army, Elvis gave Anita a car. It wasn't a flashy one, nor was it the very latest model, but it was given with a spirit of generosity that is borne out in everything Elvis does. He knew Anita didn't have a car, and he knew he wasn't going to be around to ride her in one of his. In short, he knew she needed a car, so he gave her one.

It is common knowledge how wonderfully Elvis treats his family. Nothing is too good for them. Houses, automobiles, clothes—all have been given and given freely.

Once he gave his mother a collection of expensive hats. She kept a few and gave the rest to friends. He gave her a pink Cadillac and she treasured it, not because it was big and expensive, but because it was a gift from her son.

Obedience and manners are two gifts Elvis gives

to his family that cannot be measured in dollars and cents. He addresses all his elders respectfully, and has obeyed his parents' wishes that he never drink or smoke.

But the best of all gifts Elvis can give to his family is his time, of which he came to have less and less as more money and more fame came in.

He has been as generous as possible with it. He nearly always rushed home at the end of an engagement, and while in the Army has his family as close as is allowed.

As Elvis puts it: "I just enjoy having my family around. I don't look at it as just a duty—something I ought to do. I love them and like them and I like to have them around. Doesn't everybody else feel the same way? I like to do what I can. We didn't have nothin' before—nothin' but a hard way to go."

That's Elvis Presley's story—the story he doesn't want told.

6 WHY ELVIS IS OFTEN LONELY

Elvis Presley sauntered into the studio commissary in Hollywood and slumped into a chair. Lunching with him were his cousin, Gene Smith, and Cliff Gleaves, a former Memphis disc jockey who is a hometown buddy of Elvis's.

"I'm real beat," Elvis sighed. "I didn't get much sleep last night. I didn't get home until daylight. By that time, it was hardly worth the trouble to take my clothes off."

Gene and Cliff exchanged glances and ordered lunch, but Elvis showed no interest in the menu. He invariably ate the same lunch every day—mashed potatoes with gravy, sauerkraut, crisp bacon and two glasses of milk. Knowing this, the waitress brought him out of his daydream with, "Your usual, Mr. Presley?"

"No, honey," Elvis told her. "I don't think I want anything today." He seemed more thoughtful than usual, and his eyes wandered from table to table. "Maybe," he suddenly decided, "I'll have one of those fruit gelatins with whipped cream on it."

When she was gone, he sat drumming his fingers on the table and reflecting on the night before. Once again, what promised to be a wonderful evening had turned out like so many others recently.

It is rather an odd thing to say of the young idol of millions, but for all his fame, Elvis has a problem with girls. (This has been true both in civilian life and in the Army, but this story is based on his civilian experiences, which are likely to be repeated soon.) Wherever he goes, he attracts girls—plenty of them. They write loving notes in lipstick on his white Cadillacs; they swoon as he rocks 'n' rolls on the nation's screens and stages. They send him presents by the carload. For Elvis, meeting girls has always been the easy part. But getting to know them better is something else again.

The irony is that the very fame that attracts girls to Elvis and gives him easy entree to their affections also sets up barriers that prevent the usual healthy relationships from flourishing.

The result is that, though he romances more girls in a month than most fellows his age date in a year, Elvis Presley is the loneliest guy in show business.

Unlike other young men who ask a girl out, then spend an uncomplicated afternoon or evening together seeing a movie, dancing, horseback riding, picnicking or swimming, when Elvis dates he usually finds himself the center of a mob scene, with everything short of klieg lights thrown in.

Privacy with a girl is something he can scarcely remember.

Seeing movies is perhaps Elvis's favorite pastime, yet what happens when he escorts a girl there? From the moment they walk into the theatre lobby everything and everyone seems to conspire to spoil it for him. The word spreads as if by shortwave radio that he is in the theatre, and minutes later his fans descend upon them. Any idea he might have cherished of holding hands with his girl in the back row suddenly becomes impossible in the confusion that follows. Time after time, Elvis and his date have had to elbow their way out without seeing the picture.

Taking a young lady to dinner is the same thing all over again. In restaurants, he's recognized even before they have a chance to order; fans appear as if by magic and so completely surround him that Elvis and his date usually have to leave without eating. It's the same whenever and wherever he goes with a girl. There's rarely a chance for small talk or to get to know each other better. Unfortunately for Elvis, it leaves much to be desired.

The upshot is that if Elvis is ever to be alone with a girl, he has to resort to a most unusual kind of courtship when in Hollywood. An evening he spent with Jana Lund, a pretty starlet who appeared with him in *Jailhouse Rock,* is more Elvis's rule for dating than the exception.

Elvis called at Jana's home in one of his Cadillacs around 7 that evening. They had met on the set and exchanged good-natured banter, but this was to be the first time he would be alone with her.

"What would you like to do?" Elvis asked Jana as he headed his car into Hollywood.

"There's a new band at the Palladium," she suggested. Elvis weighed the possibility of going dancing in the crowd, and quickly ruled it out with, "We'd never get past the front door." They settled on a movie and Elvis drove to a theatre on Wilshire Boulevard. "When we get there," Elvis told Jana, "walk as fast as you can up to the door and wait while I get the tickets. Maybe no one will notice."

That's just what Jana did. When they walked into the bright glare of the theatre marquee lights, she hurried to the door while Elvis hurried to the ticket window. But their movie ended before it began. By the time he had the tickets in his hand and joined her, several fans were already fast on his heels. Inside the theatre, a crowd collected around them. Elvis and Jana escaped through a side exit and made their way back to the car.

"See what I mean?" Elvis said.

The evening had just begun and the question was still: what to do? While mulling the problem, Elvis started driving out Wilshire Boulevard toward the ocean. Hours later, they were still driving about with no special destination.

On the way to Santa Monica, Elvis told Jana about his early life in the South, his family and the $100,000 home he bought for them just outside Memphis. As they drove up the coast toward Malibu Beach, Jana told Elvis many things about herself. How she has practically grown up in show business, is now making recordings and wants to be a really good singer, as well as an actress.

Still driving and talking, Elvis headed the car back for Hollywood. They passed the Sunset Strip and its glittering nightclubs, but there was no talk of visiting one. Both knew it was out of the question. So Elvis kept driving and turned on to the vast network of roads that is the Freeway. An hour later, they found themselves in Pasadena.

It was midnight by now, and they had been driving almost steadily for nearly five hours. Elvis suggested that they go to a drive-in for coffee and Cokes. They sat in the car and ordered, but with the coffee, came a dozen fans they didn't order. The waitress couldn't resist telling the gang inside about her famous customer outside. So Jana and Elvis gulped down their food and he headed the car back onto the Freeway.

This time they drove south toward Anaheim and Disneyland. Jana flicked on the car radio and sang with the music for Elvis. "Hey, you're good," he told her. "Really good." Then one of Elvis's records came up and he sang with the radio for Jana as they rolled along.

"I don't sing," he laughed. "I yell."

About 1 a.m. Elvis turned the car around and headed back for Hollywood, still talking, laughing and singing. He was beginning to relax with a girl he wanted to know better. At 2 o'clock Jana suggested that maybe she should be going home, but Elvis insisted on driving a little longer. They eventually arrived at Jana's front door around 3:30 a.m.

A conservative estimate of the distance Elvis covered that night with Jana, practically non-stop, would be approximately 300 miles. Yet driving has practically come to be Elvis's only solution to being alone with a girl.

After that, Elvis had other dates with Jana and they finally saw several movies together. But they were private screenings he had set up at the studio projection room for himself, Jana and a few of his friends. As he continued to date in Hollywood, more often than not Elvis spent the evening driving the highways and the Freeway.

As Elvis's success continued to snowball, his personal privacy—even on a date—became more and more of a problem. Like most fellows his age, he yearns for the feeling of belonging. To be identified with a close circle of friends and girls who like him for himself—not because of the sure-fire publicity that surrounds every girl he takes out more than once. But he's learned, too, that the higher he climbs, the greater his problem—and the resultant loneliness.

"I sure do get lonesome and blue," he said not

long ago. "Chill Wills told me that the bigger you get to be, the lonelier you get. I guess that's right."

At first, Elvis thought it was because he was separated so often from his family and the friends he grew up with in Memphis. But many of those friends formed the entourage that accompanied him everywhere. And several times he arranged for his family to be with him in Hollywood. It helped, but it wasn't the answer to much of his loneliness.

Elvis Presley seemingly has the world on a string. But talking with him, you can't escape the feeling that there's something important missing in his life.

Even though he seems to know what he wants, Elvis still hasn't found it. Not complete fulfillment. He never gets the opportunity others take for granted, like getting to know any girl well enough.

"Why are you lonely?" we asked Elvis. "You have plenty of girl friends. Your family and pals are often with you."

Elvis nodded his head in agreement. "I don't know exactly," he said. "I guess maybe I'm lonely for home. But it's a funny thing," he added sadly. "When I get home, after a week or so I'm itchin' to go again. But some day, I reckon, I'll settle down."

Until then, Elvis may continue to cover the miles of highway week after week, with a pretty girl beside him. Elvis is indeed lonely.

7 ELVIS PERSONALLY ANSWERS HIS CRITICS
by Bob Thomas

A lady columnist of mature years once attended a Hollywood party at which Elvis Presley was present. Now, the lady had never met Elvis and had taken some slaps at him in her column, so she wasn't sure what kind of a reaction she would get.

"But you look so young, ma'am!" Elvis commented when they met. Needless to say, the gal became a Presley fan right then and there.

"The boy is not only complimentary, he's downright charming," she said later. "He's not at all what I expected. He talks like a gentleman and he's got that honest, Southern appeal.

"And I felt that way even after I learned that he had told several other ladies at the party how young they looked. I don't care. He's wonderful."

That's the kind of reaction Elvis attracted in Hollywood. Folks who meet him invariably comment on what a nice young gentleman he is. Their surprise is understandable because Elvis Presley has been perhaps one of the most maligned entertainers in recent show biz history.

Elvis gets it from all sides. He is attacked in pulpits. He is sniped at by columnists. Politicians have even had their innings. Other entertainers deride him.

"Nobody likes him but the youngsters," said one Hollywood observer. "And maybe one of the reasons they like him so much is because some adults don't."

What does Elvis think about all this criticism? I thought it would be interesting to find out, so I arranged a date when he was in Hollywood making *Loving You*.

The scene was the Paramount commissary. The place was filled with the usual quota of stars—Shirley Booth, Anthony Quinn, James Cagney, Shirley MacLaine, Cornel Wilde—but it was Elvis who caused all the commotion when he walked in. He walked through the room almost shyly, clad in conservative gray slacks, sport shirt and white leather jacket.

He ordered a simple lunch—mashed potatoes and gravy, sauerkraut and coffee. "Can't eat much when I'm working in the picture in the afternoon," he explained. "My stomach'll show."

The pleasantries out of the way, I started tossing some anti-Presley statements his way to see if I could get a reaction. He reacted all right.

First was a report from Mexico City that he had been banned from appearing in any government-owned place because his singing "lacked esthetic values and is pornographic."

"Why, they're acting like I was getting ready to appear down there," he replied. "I don't have any plans to sing in Mexico. I might go there; I'll sing anyplace they tell me.

"Pornographic? I don't rightfully know what that means. But if it means obscene, it just ain't true. That's something I've had to fight all the time. People claim I do bumps and grinds. Why, I never did a bump or grind in my life.

"I've been to the burlesque show. I know what bumps and grinds are. But I'd never do them. I couldn't live with myself if I did. Why, I'd never think of putting on an obscene show for teenagers! If I thought I was, I'd quit. If you sow the bad seed, you've got to reap the result. I'd never be a party to putting on a dirty show."

Another comment on Elvis came from no less a source than Bing Crosby, the dean of the crooners. Here's what Bing told Dave Kaufman of *Daily Variety*:

"Presley has a pretty good beat and he sings a tune. But he needs more training and more diversified material. I can't see where he's advanced much in the past year. He should be learning other kinds of songs; he should learn how to talk; how to act in sketches. He's a good-looking kid. Frank Sinatra, Perry Como, all of us learned as we came along to work in sketches with comedians, with girls, how to time jokes. But Elvis just slouches.

"The next couple of years will tell whether he's just a fad. You can't just sing 'Hound Dog' all the time, and his tunes all sound like it. I think he's a sexy-looking kid and can do very well in his career if he makes the most of the opportunity. But he has to take those sideburns off and do other things.

"The kids will like him all the more if he's smart and segues (makes a transition) into something else. For a change of pace, he should try comedy songs, Westerns, everything else. A guy singing one kind of song isn't going to last long."

Elvis read the article and then smiled, "All I can say is, he ought to know."

But in his own defense, he said he was doing different kinds of songs now. With "Love Me Tender," he proved he could do ballads. And he's trying new things all the time.

Does he slouch?

"Well, I don't know," he grinned. "I do just sorta stand the way I'm most comfortable."

What about the sideburns?

"They ain't a-comin' off," Elvis said emphatically. "I've grown used to them and I like 'em," he said. "I've been wearing them ever since I was a kid—when I only had a little white fuzz up there."

He told the story of how he happened to become such a fan of sideburns:

"My Dad was a truck driver and truck drivers were my idols. That was the thing I wanted most to be in the world.

"We used to live near the highway in Tupelo, Mississippi. I'd see those truck drivers with their shirts off, handkerchiefs around their necks and wearing sideburns and moustaches. I thought they were great. My ambition was to look like them and drive a big rig. I don't see much sense in shaving them off now. They're sort of a trademark with me, so why fool around with success?"

He admitted he might have to shave them off for Uncle Sam. "Nobody in the Army has ever avoided getting a close haircut," he reasoned.

Getting back to Bing, Elvis commented, "I'm learning all the time. You can't pick up everything in this business all at once. When he [Crosby] started out, he had to learn it all, too."

Bing had commented that he had never met Elvis, but would like to. Elvis said he'd sure like to meet Bing, too.

One of the things that amazes Elvis is the way the columnists treat his love life.

"You take a girl out twice and all of a sudden you're engaged to marry her," he exclaimed. I've never even thought about getting married," he said flatly. "To tell the truth, I've never had time to. I've been so busy in the past year or two that I haven't had time to do anything but my work."

The enthusiastic Presley following has been much

criticized as being wild, senseless youth. Elvis came out in stout defense of his fans. "Sure, they get a little enthusiastic," he said, "but I've never had a destructive crowd. They've never torn up the seats or ruined the theatre or anything like that.

"Adults don't understand those kids. When you're young, you've got a lot of energy and enthusiasm. You've got to blow it off somehow. That's what kids do when they see my shows. Later, when they grow up, they'll lose a lot of that energy and they'll act like grownups.

"I've got to admit that I get a big kick out of watching them. Sure, they get a little rambunctious sometimes. You could do things to control them, but when you try to control too much, you spoil some of their enjoyment. Part of the show is for them to let themselves go."

Elvis said the most fun he has in show business is doing personal appearances. "I don't like to go out on the road for a month, because that wears you out," he said. "But to go out for five days is really fun. You see new places and meet new people and have an exciting time."

He admitted that personals can be pretty hazardous.

"I've never been really seriously hurt," he said, "but I've had my hair pulled and gotten a few scratches. And I've lost a few suits of clothes."

The closest shave came one night in Kansas City, Missouri, he recalled. He was finishing up his last song and trying to act nonchalant so the crowd wouldn't notice that he was getting ready for his exit. But the kids knew the show was ending and they made a rush for Elvis.

"Everybody was hysterical, including me," he said. "The last thing I remember was someone saying, 'We've got to get you out of here.' Then two hands reached out of the crowd and picked me up and carried me all the way to the exit."

The personal appearances are now well handled, as far as security matters are concerned, he said. There are no fewer than 30 to guard his entrance and exit.

After personals, he likes doing movies best. He's humble about his own abilities and admits he has a lot to learn about the picture business. Chances are, he'll get a lot of chance to learn.

He appeared to be least happy with television as a medium, and that's understandable. Elvis made his first big hit on the Dorsey Brothers show. Then he did a spot with Milton Berle and that's when he drew a barrage of criticism for his gyrations.

When he appeared with Steve Allen, he was required to wear evening clothes and avoid movement. "I wasn't too happy with that," he admitted.

He liked working with Ed Sullivan, though he didn't seem pleased with the way the cameras shot him only from the waist up on the last show. "Sometimes in a rehearsal they will shoot you one way and then it'll be different when the show goes on," he said. He's now through with his commitments with

Sullivan; no doubt he'll have more control over how he is presented on TV in the future.

Like the lady columnist, I came away with a different impression of Elvis Presley from the one some of his detractors try to paint. He's an earnest young guy who seems to have a real loyalty to his fans and a desire to grow as a performer. He's soft-spoken, never brash, as you might expect him to be.

He doesn't criticize other performers, which is a common practice among show biz people. He's polite and respectful, yet it's obvious he's getting a whale of a kick out of life.

His level-headedness was illustrated by his view of the future:

"I've never tried to plan ahead or try to foresee what I'll be doing in the future. I take each day as it comes and try to do my best and grow in this business. So far, everything has gone pretty well; I just hope things continue that way."

8 THINGS YOU NEVER KNEW ABOUT ELVIS
by Paul Denis

Elvis Presley wanted so much to give his mother a mink coat, but she never wanted one. But the great pink Cadillac he gave her she really liked, and rode in it whenever she went out of the house.

The mansion he bought for his parents has a picture of Jesus over the ivory organ.

As an identical twin whose brother had died at birth, he always wanted a brother and a sister.

He likes Ski Pool, a variation of French Pool, so much that he bought the game and installed it in his house.

He's a good boxer, but doesn't like to talk about it because it might encourage troublemakers who want to prove something.

He likes to try all the skill games at an amusement

park, and has good muscular coordination.

He likes to read newspaper and magazine stories about himself, and is sensitive to criticism. But, as he grows older, he is calmer about some of the fantastic and utterly untrue accusations made against him.

He still likes teddy bears and little dogs. When his parents moved into the new mansion, he installed on the grounds horses, mules, chickens and dogs.

He likes bright colors in his clothes because, when he's in a low mood, they give him a lift. He's fussy, but not fanatical, about his clothes.

He's wild about motorcycles and refused to permit Hal Wallis to put a clause in their seven-year movie contract forbidding motorcycle riding.

When he made his TV network debut on *Stage Show* he was described as a "combination of Frankie Laine, Johnnie Ray and Tony Martin." Now the critics admit he is like nobody else.

He has a fine memory. He's memorized things he likes, such as General MacArthur's farewell address and the Gettysburg Address. He remembers at least a part of every song he's ever heard.

He likes to carry a fat roll of money with him, and often forgets it in dressing rooms. So his associates always check dressing rooms and hotel suites before they leave.

He likes to nap for an hour after a personal appearance—that's how much vigor he puts into his performance.

He wants to be everybody's friend, and he can't

understand why the press has been against him. He was genuinely shocked when the press accused him of being obscene. And he can't understand why newspapers have him courting every girl he looks at.

He still has a lot of energy, and says: "When I was a kid, I used to play football for hours and hours, and never feel tired."

He doesn't like to perform in nightclubs because "The people are eating when I come on. . . . An audience like this can't show appreciation."

He says some day he wants to write a book about how it feels to be an entertainer: "It's tough, man, tough."

He likes to visit penny arcades at amusement parks, fairs or wherever he happens to find them.

He keeps a scrapbook at home but pastes in only "nice things they say about me."

Because he was an only child, he was not permitted to go out of the house alone and play with the other kids. "I didn't play away from the house until I was 15," he says.

Sometimes, when he's really tired, he'll set up a projection machine, throw an old movie on the ceiling, and lie in bed and watch. He relaxes that way.

He says the girls did not go for him when he was in high school, and that he was "no big wheel!" as a student.

He sang with his parents in the choir of the Pentecostal Assembly of God church. His mother's favorite hymn was "Take My Hand, Precious Lord."

He sang freely for relatives, but in high school he appeared in only two school shows. He wasn't sure he was good enough to appear in public.

He enjoys listening to "good religious singing quartets."

He started wearing sideburns at 16, when he thought sideburns and a mustache would make him look older. (But he wasn't able to raise a mustache.)

He doesn't like sideburns any more, but hesitated to trim them for fear his fans would resent it. (The Army, of course, took care of that!)

He still likes to travel, and hates staying in any one place too long.

He likes best, from among his own records, "Don't Be Cruel."

He still regrets he never met the late Jimmy Dean, saying, "It was a real tragedy he died so young."

He is "self-assured" rather than conceited, according to Richard Egan, who worked with him in *Love Me Tender*.

The Bible he won at 11, for singing in church, is still in his house.

He always worried about his parents. To this day, he becomes frightened when his father dives into a swimming pool for fear he won't come up.

He once spent $750 in one night at an amusement park, mostly at games where he threw baseballs at bottles.

His oldest (though not in age) girl friend is Barbara Hearn, whose friendship goes back to 1953.

In his personal life, he does everything on impulse, like most young people.

Steve Allen said he's "a very solid performer, and will be around a lot longer than his detractors think."

He likes his hair to be just right, and will comb it 15 minutes before a personal appearance.

He is restless, and drives himself hard in his work.

He likes most Southern dishes, except hominy. He likes to eat between meals. He nibbles peanuts and popcorn on a movie set.

He wears bright-colored silk pajamas, both top and bottom, and likes to sleep in a big bed.

He refuses to fake his singing for publicity photos; he insists on singing and playing his guitar while the photos are being taken.

He refused to pose with a death mask of James Dean, explaining he admired Dean so much he didn't "want to cheapen his memory" and "I don't want to cash in on the poor guy."

He averages 40 minutes on stage on personal appearances, but when audiences dig him, he'll stay on longer.

When he's performing, he wears an extra-large suit and shirt, to keep the buttons and seams from tearing.

His grandfather always wanted him to become a preacher.

He once said, "I don't mind being controversial. . . . Even Jesus wasn't loved by everyone in his day."

He believes girls like him to look sullen, brooding,

menacing. That's why he tries not to smile in photos.

His bedroom at home has a mirror covering one entire wall, with dark blue walls, black bedspread trimmed in white leather, and white rug.

He doesn't think he looks good when he laughs. Doesn't think he has the right kind of teeth and a broad enough smile.

When he can't drive someplace, he prefers going by train. He avoids air travel since a near-accident a few years ago when a plane he was flying in almost crashed.

When he graduated from high school in 1953, his ambition was to get a job as a policeman when he became 21.

His favorite food is eggs fried hard on both sides; bacon fried hard; pork chops, toast and fruit.

The good-night snack he likes most consists of peanut butter and mashed bananas on white bread with a glass of milk or Pepsi-Cola. This has been a favorite of his for years.

He was on a black-and-pink kick when he was 20. He had a black-and-pink Cadillac, black-and-pink shirts, etc., and then got tired of it all.

Although he won a first prize and a fifth prize in amateur singing contests, he never got any money from singing until his recording of "That's All Right" turned into a hit

His ambition always was "to be somebody and to feel like somebody." Today he yearns above all to be a successful actor, because "singers come and go, and they die out."

He can play piano as well as guitar.

He has cost the government $500,000 a year in lost taxes during his Army period.

Printed in Great Britain
by Amazon